Robin French

Gilbert is Dead

Methuen Drama

Published by Methuen Drama 2009

1 3 5 7 9 10 8 6 4 2

Methuen Drama
A & C Black Publishers Limited
36 Soho Square
London W1D 3QY
www.acblack.com

Copyright © 2009 by Robin French

Robin French has asserted his rights under the
Copyright, Designs and Patents Act 1988
to be identified as the author of this work

ISBN: 978 1 408 12778 0

A CIP catalogue record for this book is available from
the British Library

Typeset by Country Setting, Kingsdown, Kent

*shining*man
presents

Gilbert is Dead

by Robin French

First performance at Hoxton Hall, London,
on 4th November 2009

Sign language interpreted performance on 17th November

The production runs approximately 2 hours,
including a 15-minute interval

The script is correct at time of going to press,
though some changes may have been made during rehearsals

Supported by Unity Theatre Trust

LOTTERY FUNDED

Gilbert is Dead

by Robin French

LUCIUS TRICKETT	Ronan Vibert
LUCILLE TRICKETT	Kate Burdette
BARTHOLOMEW MERIWETHER	William Chubb
MAISY FELLOWS	Suzan Sylvester

Director	Robert Wolstenholme
Producer	Ben Crystal
Designer	Christopher Hone
Lighting Designer	Rob Mills
Puppet Maker	Seonaid Goody
Illustrator	Ian Bass
Fight Director	Tim Klotz
Composer	Nick Gill
Company Manager	Kate Schofield
Stage Manager	Sophie Cable
Assistant Stage Manager	Sarah Chapman
Board Operator	Ryan Harding
Costume Supervisor	Hannah Gibbs
Artist / Model Maker	Jewelfloozy
Model Maker	Bryony Rumble
Marketing Assistant	Alison Fraser
Production Photographer	Scott Wishart
Sign Language Interpreter	Donna Ruane
Historical Consultant	Kate Williams
Publicity	Sue Hyman Associates Ltd
	t 020 7379 8420
	www.suehyman.com

With thanks to

Mary Fitzgerald, Joe Hutton, Debs Medworth and Aude Powell, Siva Zagel and all at Hoxton Hall, Ben Hall and Lily Williams at Curtis Brown, Elinor Hilton, Kettners, 1Click, Charlotte Loveridge and all at Methuen, John Wiltshire and Lisa Moore at TicketWeb, Michael Orford and Jeffrey Goh at Bowker Orford, Emma Mottram and BAC, Tim Roseman at Theatre 503, Sasha Regan at Union Theatre, Donmar Warehouse, Rose Bruford College, The Prince Arthur Pub, Kate Duffy at EUSA, Piers Mason at Impact, Richard Gresham at WhatsOnStage, Derren Brown, Phillis Dorris, Alexis at London Taxidermy, Mike Elsey at Jumbo Colour, Nathan Woodhead, Russell Hosley and Martin Dunn of the British Historical Taxidermy Society, Simon David at the Royal Court Theatre bookshop and Jon, Mole, Dave, Vanessa, Nicola at Bacchus Pub and Kitchen

J.J. at JogPost.co.uk. For every 1000 flyers distributed, JogPost are planting two trees

Ian Rimmington, Johnny Hay, James Hadley and Oliver Bliss at the Arts Council

Harry Landis and Andreas Michaelides at Unity Theatre Trust

Fiona Davis of Fiona Davis Costume Designs and Ruth Bagnall at www.costumia.co.uk

Ben and Duncan Mee and Aly Alkhersan of Dartmoor Zoological Park, www.dartmoorzoologicalpark.co.uk

Mike Bradwell, Abigail Gonda, Jane Fallowfield, Jonathan Coy, Robin Samson, Hattie Morahan, Jackie Kane, Nick Malinowski, Neil Sheppeck, Lucy Smith, Seth Rook Williams, Adrian Gee, Alan Valentine, Adam Russ, Bert and Bertie, Gail Downey at WearDowney, Russell Sage and Francesca Findlater, Jos Grain, Lou Cannon, Ysabel Clare, Olivia Bennett, Jamie Harding and Jessica Davey

and the *shining*man Angels, without whom . . .

Archangels
David and Hilary Crystal

Cherubs
Surestate Ltd

Seraphs
Adam Simmonds
Audrey Norman

Cast

KATE BURDETTE   Lucille Trickett

Kate studied English Literature at Bristol University, then trained at The Poor School, London.

Theatre includes: *Where There's a Will* directed by Sir Peter Hall, Hermia in *A Midsummer Nights Dream* and Kitty in *Charley's Aunt* (Bristol Shakespeare Festival), Sibyl in *Private Lives* (Margate Theatre Royal) and most recently playing The Girl in *The Man Outside* (Haymarket Theatre Royal).

TV includes: *The Debt*, and Stephen Poliakoff's *Capturing Mary*.

Film includes: Lady Harriett in *The Duchess*, Isabelle in *The Dark Side of the Earth*. Kate is due to start work on the upcoming feature film *Catwalk*.

WILLIAM CHUBB   Bartholomew Meriwether

Theatre includes: *Love's Labour's Lost* (Rose Theatre, Kingston); *The Sea, Hay Fever* (Theatre Royal Haymarket), *The History Boys* (National Theatre in the West End and tour), *Galileo's Daughter, Don Juan, Man and Superman, Design for Living, Fight for Barbara* (Peter Hall Company), *You Never Can Tell* (Theatre Royal Bath, Garrick Theatre London & Tour), *Whose Life is it Anyway?* (Comedy Theatre), *Justifying War: Scenes from The Hutton Enquiry* (Tricycle Theatre), *Homebody Kabul* (Cheek by Jowl/Young Vic), *A Raisin in the Sun* (Young Vic), *Ghosts* (English Touring Theatre), *Burning Issues* (Hampstead Theatre), *He Stumbled, Judith* (both Wrestling School), *Tulip Futures* (Soho Theatre), *The School Mistress* (Chichester Festival Theatre), *Time and the Conways* (Old Vic). For the National Theatre: *The London Cuckolds, The Invention of Love, The Princes' Play, The Madness of King George III* (also New York), *Trelawney of the Wells*. For the RSC: *Conversation, The Silent Woman, Three Sisters, The New Inn, The Taming of the Shrew, Julius Caesar, The Merchant of Venice*. For Cheek by Jowl: *The Man of Mode, A Midsummer Night's Dream*.

Film includes: *Veer, Gladiatress, Mrs Caldicot's Cabbage War, The Affair of the Necklace, Milk, The Woodlanders*.

Television includes: *The Montagu Trial, Absolute Power, Cherished, Trial and Retribution, Midsomer Murders, Murder in Mind, Heartbeat, A & E III, Relic Hunter, Active Defence, Playing the Field, Randall & Hopkirk Deceased, Extremely Dangerous, Rocket to the Moon, The Ambassador* (Series 1 & 2), *Breakout, Kavanagh QC, To Play the King, House of Cards, The Buddha of Suburbia, Sleepers, Signs and Wonders, Just Us*.

Radio includes: *The Invention of Love, The Pimlico Poisoner, Twelfth Night*.

SUZAN SYLVESTER Maisy Fellows

Suzan trained at Central School of Speech and Drama.

Theatre includes: *Negative Space* (New End Theatre), *3 Sisters on Hope Street, Terms of Abuse* (both Hampstead Theatre), *Othello* (Salisbury Playhouse), *Heartbreak House* (Watford), *Frankie and Johnny in the Clair de Lune* (Sound Theatre), *Tabloid Caligula* (Arcola Theatre, London and 59th Street, New York), *Black Milk, Terrorism* and *Cleansed* (Royal Court), *Crooked, Little Baby Nothing, Shang-a-Lang* and *Cardboys* (The Bush Theatre), *The Real Thing* (tour), *The Secret Rapture* and *Three Sisters* (Chichester), *Betrayal* (Northcott, Exeter), *The Reckless are Dying Out* (Lyric Hammersmith); *The House of Bernarda Alba* (Theatr Clwyd), *All My Sons, The Glass Menagerie, Romeo and Juliet* and *An Enemy of the People* (Young Vic, which transferred to The Playhouse), *As You Like It, The Seagull* and *The Government Inspector* (Crucible Theatre), *Kindertransport* and *Yiddish Trojan Women* (Soho Theatre), *Life is a Dream* (West Yorkshire Playhouse), *Pericles* and *All's Well That Ends Well* (RSC) and *'Tis a Pity She's a Whore, A Small Family Business* and *A View From the Bridge* (National Theatre, which transferred to The Aldwych and for which she won the Olivier Award for best newcomer).

Film includes: *Streets of Yesterday* and *Bilingual*.

Television includes: *Kingdom, EastEnders, Holby City, Silent Witness, The Quatermass Experiment, Doctors, Family Affairs, The Bill, Casualty, Where the Heart is, Maisie Raine, A Touch of Frost, London's Burning, Holding On, Wycliffe, Pie in the Sky, Peak Practice, Rides, Misterioso* and *Call Me Mister*.

Radio includes: *Macbeth, Pentacost, The Rover* and *The Last Dare*.

RONAN VIBERT Lucius Trickett

Theatre includes: *Dying For It* (Almeida), *Uncle Vanya* (Wilton's Music Hall), *A Midsummer Night's Dream* (Bristol Old Vic), *Antarctica* (Savoy Theatre*)*, *The Mother, War and Peace* and *A Matter of Life and Death* (National Theatre), *Hello and Goodbye* (Theatr Clwyd), *The Yiddish Trojan Women* (Soho Theatre), *Peer Gynt* (Thelma Holt Productions), *Walpurgis Night* (Gate Theatre), *The Debutante Ball* (Hampstead Theatre), *Amongst Barbarians* (Royal Exchange & Hampstead), *The Chinese Wolf, More Light,* and *Making Noise Quietly* (Bush Theatre).

Film includes: *Shanghai* (Weinstein Company), *Beowulf & Grendel* (Spice Factory), *Tristan and Isolde* (Scott Free), *Gladiatress* (Mission), *Tombraider II* (Paramount), *The Pianist* (Rennes Film), *The Cat's Meow* (Lionsgate), *Killing Me Softly* (Montecito Pictures), *Shadow of a Vampire* (Lionsgate*)*, *The Grass Arena* (BBC Films), *Sammy and Rosie Get Laid* (Working Title).

Television includes: *Poirot: A Three Act Tragedy. The Bill , Lewis, The Sarah Jane Adventures, Lead Balloon, Hotel Babylon, Taggart, Rome, Midsomer Murders, Ultimate Force IV, Hex, Waking The Dead, Peter Ackroyd's London, Mary Shelley, Keen Eddie, The Scarlet Pimpernel, Tales From The Crypt, Between The Lines, The Buccaneers, Jeeves and Wooster, Traffik*.

Creative Team

ROBIN FRENCH   Writer

Studied modern and medieval languages at Cambridge University and playwriting on the Royal Court Young Writers' Programme.

Plays include: *Bear Hug* (Royal Court Theatre Upstairs and subsequent productions in Italy, Germany, Ireland and Poland), *Africa* and *Pigeon* (Flight 5065 on the London Eye), and *Breakfast Hearts/Choirplay* (Theatre 503).

Robin was chosen by *The Observer* as one of the country's most promising talents and is currently under commission from Paines Plough.

ROBERT WOLSTENHOLME   Director

Studied Theatre at Warwick University and Directing at Drama Studio, London and on the National Theatre Studio Directors' Programme.

As director/co-producer: shiningman's *One Minute* (Courtyard), *Guerilla/Whore* (Tabard), *Here* (Tristan Bates), *Private Lives* (Canal Café) and *Closer* (Landor).

As director: *The Unattended* (Gilded Balloon, Edinburgh), *This to This* (Union and Colour House Theatres), *Gift* and *If No One Loves You, Change* (King's Head), *Bash* (Hen & Chickens), *Road* (Croydon Clocktower), *Love & Understanding* and *Can't Stand Up For Falling Down* (Etcetera), *Christie In Love* and *Oedipus The King* (Young Vic Genesis Directors' Project), *Octopus Pie* (Landor and Edinburgh), *Dracula* (Drayton Court), *Mother Tongue* (Oval House), *A Snow Scene* and *Sleeping Nightie* (White Bear), *The Razorblade Cuckoo* (Link Theatre), *Can You Keep a Secret?* and *Was He Anyone?* (Croydon Youth Theatre); numerous rehearsed readings including for the Bush, at Soho Theatre for Amnesty International and for Old Vic/New Voices.

As assistant or associate director: work at the Old Red Lion, the Finborough, the Green Room (Manchester), the Donmar Warehouse and the Almeida At Home, in the West End and on tour.

Robert is about to direct Anthony Neilson's *The Night Before Christmas* (Hen & Chickens, 1-19th December) and Simon Vinnicombe's *Make Me a Martyr* (forthcoming, June–July 2010, see www.shiningman.co.uk for more details).

BEN CRYSTAL   Producer

Studied English Language and Linguistics at Lancaster University, then Acting at Drama Studio, London.

As producer: shiningman's *One Minute* (Courtyard) and Simon Vinnicombe's *Make Me a Martyr* (forthcoming, June–July 2010).

As actor, theatre includes: shiningman's *One Minute* (Courtyard), *5pm, No Particular Afternoon* (The Space), *Ohio Impromptu* and *Rough for Theatre 2* (Capital Centre), *Caligula* (Union Theatre), *Comedy of Errors* and *Titus Andronicus* (Shakespeare's Globe), *Twelfth Night* (national tour), *Christie In Love* (Young Vic Genesis Directors' Project) and countless rehearsed readings and development workshops.

TV includes: *Holby City*, *The Bill* and *Starting Out*.

Film includes: Julian Wald in *Uprising* (NBC/Warner) and the independents *Notes, Hero, Click, Mercy* and *Cupid's Whores*.

He is a prolific narrator/voiceover artist. His narration work includes: Audiobooks for RNIB Talking Books, including *A Clockwork Orange*, and narration for Channel 4 and the BBC.

Ben has written three books about Shakespeare - including *Shakespeare's Words* (Penguin) and *Shakespeare on Toast* (Icon) - and regularly teaches and leads workshops on the bard.

For more details, see www.bencrystal.com

CHRISTOPHER HONE   Designer

Studied Theatre Design at Nottingham Trent University.

Theatre includes: *Coyote Ugly, Italian American Reconciliation* & *The Time of Your Life* (Finborough Theatre), *The Lesson, Vincent in Brixton, Romeo and Juliet, A Taste of Honey* & *Othello* (International Tours), *One Minute* (Courtyard Theatre), *Here* (Tristan Bates), *Guerilla/Whore* (Tabard), *Dorian Gray* (Leicester Square Theatre) and is currently working on *Miracles* (Covent Garden) and will design *shining*man's *Make Me a Martyr* (June–July 2010).

TV includes: the complete studio re-design of QVC, Big Brother, Celebrity Big Brother, Hollyoaks and numerous commercials.

For more details, see www.honedesigns.com

ROB MILLS   Lighting Designer

As Lighting Designer, theatre includes: *Hayton on Homicide* (The Space UK & Tristan Bates Theatre), *Love Bites* (Leatherhead Theatre), *Footlights/Oxford Review/Durham Review* (Cambridge Arts Theatre), *Romeo and Juliet* (Cambridge Arts Theatre), *Cambridge University Annual Fashion Show* (The Corn Exchange, Cambridge), *The Elixir of Love* (Stanley Hall Opera), *The Seagull* (ADC), *Our Town* (ADC), *Footlights 2006 National Tour*.

And as Production & Lighting Designer: *Madama Butterfly* (Harlequin Theatre & E-M Forster Theatre), *42nd Street* (Cambridge Corn Exchange), *Parade* (ADC Theatre), *Yeomen of the Guard* (as Production Designer, Minack Theatre), Savitri – (The Round Church, Cambridge), *Don Giovanni* (West Rd Concert Hall), *Crave* (C³ Edinburgh).

For more details, see: www.robwmills.co.uk

SEONAID GOODY   Puppet Maker

Trained as a puppeteer and puppet maker at Central School of Speech and Drama and as apprentice at the Little Angel Theatre.

Her work includes: *Beyond The Tracks* (Rehearsed reading for the RSC), *The Giraffe, The Pelly and Me* (The Little Angel Theatre), *Swan Lake* (Animation for San Francisco Ballet), *The Samson Project* (Bone Orchard), *Princess and the Pea* (Polka Theatre) and *Give Us A Hand!* (The Little Angel Theatre).

She has made puppets for: *A Midsummer Night's Dream* (Shakespeare's Globe), *Give Us a Hand!* (The Little Angel Theatre), *Watercolours* (Quicksilver Theatre), *Furies* (Bialystok Puppetry Festival/Baron's Court Theatre), *The Magic Carpet* (Lyric Hammersmith).

She has worked as director/puppetry director on *The Singing Bone* (Tête-à-Tête Festival at Riverside Studios and Grimeborn at The Arcola), *Jack Pratchard* (Buxton Puppet Festival 2009), *Midsummer Night's Dream* (Shakespeare's Globe), *Huh!* (Etcetera Theatre) and *The Fairy Queen* (Armonico Consort).

Seonaid has recently been nominated for the 2010 Arts Foundation Fellowship.

IAN BASS   Illustrator

Ian has illustrated for countless books and magazines. Ian drew the designs for the backcloths, the puppets, the poster and the cover of the script for *Gilbert is Dead*.

His theatre includes: productions include *A Christmas Carol*, *Into The Woods* and *Treasure Island*. He is a founding member of the band *Scales of the Unexpected*.

For more details, see www.scalesoftheunexpected.co.uk

TIM KLOTZ   Fight Director

Tim founded *YoungBlood* (a fight direction company) nine years ago, and has been working internationally as a certified fight director and instructor for over 12 years. Teaching includes Drama Centre London, Oxford School of Drama and universities and colleges around the world.

A scholar of both movement and text, his fights grow organically from the scripts he works on. His approach is unique, and is best known for his cutting edge approach to acting a fight scene.

Credits include: work at Shakespeare's Globe, Lyric Hammersmith, Royal Festival Hall, Haymarket Theatre Basingstoke, Nashville Ballet, Comedy Theatre London, and The Tobacco Factory Bristol, and for the BBC & Channel 4. He has also worked on major video games for Sony and Sega.

For more details, see www.timklotz.info

NICK GILL   Composer

Nick is a composer, musician and playwright. He produces music for theatre, installations, film, dance, live performance and for studio recordings. As well as his cross-platform work, he writes and performs with his 7-piece instrumental group *The Monroe Transfer*, as well as *Fireworks Night* and *Lights*.

Composition for theatre includes: *Thrown* (Royal Court), *England* (MeetFactory, Prague), *DNA* (Old Red Lion), *The Fall of Roderick Usher* (Riverside Studios), *Burying Your Brother In The Pavement* (New Wimbledon), *Mine* (Hampstead), *You Know Who* (Canvas Dance).

Composition for film includes: *Pandora's Box* (live accompaniment at BFI SouthBank), *Fidelity* (dir. Ortensia Visconti), *The Way In Is The Way Out* (dir. Elizabeth Hancok), *Coffee Sex You* (dir. Marcel Grant), *Wednesday Matinee Club* (dir. Rachna Suri).

Writing includes: *Mirror teeth* (Finborough Theatre), *10:15–10:19 (twice)* (Tabard), *fiji land* (Soho Theatre), *Funeralesque* (Trafalgar Studios), *heaven* and *storm/ static* (Royal Court), and short works with The Apathists (Theatre 503); supported by Peggy Ramsay Foundation for work on *broken earth & dead blue sky*.

For more details, see www.nickfuckinggill.com

KATE SCHOFIELD   Company Manager

Studied Theatre at Warwick University and Directing at London School of Music and Dramatic Arts (LAMDA).

Stage Management: includes various productions at The Gate Theatre London, Royal Court Downstairs @ The Duke of York's, Oval House, Bloomsbury's Theatre and Hackney Empire.

Director/Assistant Director: includes productions at Theatre Royal Bury St Edmunds, Northcott Theatre Exeter, The Courtyard Theatre, Jermyn Street Theatre, The Man in the Moon, The White Bear, Tabard and Tristan Bates.

As Production Coordinator: includes work on feature films, documentaries and music videos for Motion Picture House, Worlds End Productions, 20th Century Productions, Ford Films and Ilya Salkind Company.

Kate also recently spent 18 months at the Young Vic as the Assistant to Associate Artistic Director. This included administrating the Genesis Directors' Programme and assisting the production of the Jerwood Directors' Award productions.

SOPHIE CABLE   Stage Manager

Sophie trained at Central School of Speech and Drama. Her previous stage management experience includes: *Peter Pan* (Kensington Gardens), *Dimetos* (Donmar), *A Guest for Dinner* (CSSD/Punchdrunk at Arts Depot), Venue stage manager at the Pleasance Edinburgh, *Sfumato* (V&A Museum) and *N (Bonaparte)* at the Boston Centre for the Arts, USA.

For more details, see www.sophiecable.co.uk

SARAH CHAPMAN   Assistant Stage Manager

Sarah is currently completing a BFA in Stage Management at Boston University. Recent stage management credits include: *The 25th Annual Putnam County Spelling Bee* and *Chapter Two* at Theatre Aspen in Colorado; *The Oil Thief* (world premiere) at Boston Playwright's Theatre; *How I Learned to Drive*, *Pope Joan* (world premiere) and *Under Milk Wood* at Boston University. Sarah is working with *shining*man on an internship from EUSA.

RYAN HARDING   Board Operator

Work in lighting and sound includes: *This to This* (Union and Colour House Theatres), *Johnjo* and *Call Me If You Feel Too Happy* (Old Red Lion), *Torn Out Pages* (Landor), *The Union of Shorts*, *2007 Terror Season*, *Curse of the Werewolf*, *Caligula*, *Stars in the Morning Sky*, *Spring Awakening*, *412 Letters* and *Medeia* (all Union Theatre).

HANNAH GIBBS   Costume Supervisor

Hannah trained in Costume Design and Construction at Queen Margaret University in Edinburgh. Theatre work includes: *Romeo and Juliet*, *A Taste of Honey*, *Ajax* (Love and Madness), *Duet for One* (Almeida On Tour), *The Time of Your Life* (Icarus Theatre Collective, The Finborough Theatre), *A Latesummer Night's Dream* (Mill Pond Media), *Crazy for You* (Edinburgh University Footlights, The Church Hill Theatre), *The Wind in the Willows* (Queen Margaret University, Theatre Workshop), *Dick McWhittington* (The Brunton Theatre), *Troilus and Cressida* (RSC and Edinburgh International Festival, The Kings Theatre). Films include: *Libertatia*, *Daniel and Tess* (London Film School).

JEWELFLOOZY   Artist/Model Maker

Jewelfloozy is the nom d'arte of London based actor and artist Charlotte Weston, who specialises in bespoke papier-mâché creations. She has exhibited in London, Brighton and online. Charlotte helped create the animals in Lucius' taxidermy museum.

For more details, see www.myspace.com/jewelfloozy

BRYONY RUMBLE   Model Maker

Bryony is a London based visual artist, specialising in costume props/creature design and fabrication. She trained as a Technical Effects artist, and Cordwainer at The University of the Arts London.

She has worked as a designer, props and costume maker, and scenic artist for theatre, television, short films, music videos and events.

Credits include: Tartuffe Productions *A Door Must be Open or Shut* (King's Head Theatre); Jellyhead 3D (creating costumes for *Harry Hill's TV Burp*, *Al Murray's Happy Hour*); Punchdrunk's *Masque of the Red Death*, and various short films and promos for Sentinel Productions, Annex Films, JOY@RSA, and FletcherWilson. Bryony has just started working on *Harry Potter and the Deathly Hallows.*

ALISON FRASER   Marketing Assistant

Studied Modern History at the University of St Andrews.

She has worked for The Byre Theatre, St Andrews, the Barron Theatre, St Andrews, the Traverse Theatre, Edinburgh and currently works at BAC, London.

SCOTT WISHART   Production Photographer

Scott Wishart studied Photography at Staffordshire University and cut his professional teeth freelancing for many years at *The Guardian* and *The Observer* newspapers, working all over the world on travel and issue-based assignments.

He is widely published in a broad range of national and international journals and in addition to a number of major UK publishing houses, shoots portraits for EMI, Sony BMG, Decca and Universal.

Scott is also a regular contributor to *Time Out London* and worked with *shining*man on the 2008 production of *One Minute*.

For more details, see www.floatingbear.co.uk

About the Company

*shining*man
was set up in late 2007 by director Robert Wolstenholme
and producer Ben Crystal because of a shared love of text-
based theatre and a forensic attention to theatrical detail.

We produce plays that directly address contemporary
events, trends and ideologies. They can be either old or
new, but must be the best theatrical writing, with bold
vision and ambition. We produce our work to the highest
possible production values, through our dynamic and
experienced core creative team and by forming partnerships
with like-minded and gifted artists. Our next production will
be Simon Vinnicombe's *Make Me a Martyr*, June–July 2010,
a new play about disaffection and radicalisation among
British youths.

*shining*man has an active Angels' scheme. We are indebted
to, and could not continue, without such support.

If you would like to find out more about us, the Angels'
scheme, or our next production, please head to our website,
email us, or fill in the audience feedback questionnaire.

www.shiningman.co.uk
info@shiningman.co.uk

On *shining*man's 2008 revival of *One Minute*,
by Simon Stephens:

WhatsOnStage
'Stunning . . . a thoroughly entertaining
and thought-provoking production' ****

Time Out
'Colin Tierney & Ben Crystal are excellent . . . director
Robert Wolstenholme keeps the tension up throughout' ***

Simon Stephens
'There wasn't a single moment of this production I didn't believe . . .'

Hoxton Hall

Since 1863 Hoxton Hall has epitomised the spirit of Shoreditch as a visible artistic and creative presence in the community: entertaining, supporting and educating local people.

Today we work with those who are starting out. We excite talent; encourage risk-taking; supporting and advising those who wish to explore their creativity and potential.

Our unique Victorian music hall theatre inspires young people and young arts companies to experiment and create work which breaks personal and artistic boundaries.

www.hoxtonhall.co.uk
events@hoxtonhall.co.uk

Much of the taxidermy in Lucius' museum was provided by

LONDON TAXIDERMY
www.londontaxidermy.com

Gilbert is Dead

Author's Note

As a young writer, you are often encouraged to write about what you know. They're right – it probably is safer that way. I wanted to write dangerously. The best writing is personal, but that need not mean autobiographical.

This is a play about change and delusion and it affected in me quite a bit of both. I'm enormously grateful to the many patient and wise people who helped me along the way – especially Nina Steiger, Rachel Taylor, Abigail Gonda, Jenny Worton and all at Paines Plough.

I would like to thank *shining*man, and especially Bob who has believed in the play for so long.

Finally, and most of all, I'd like to thank my agent, Ben Hall, for all his hard work and support and for never ever thinking *Gilbert is Dead* was dead.

Robin French,
London, October 2009

Characters

Lucius Trickett, *a London taxidermist, forty-five*
Lucille Trickett, *his daughter, sixteen*
Bartholomew Meriwether, *a London physician, fifty-five*
Maisy Fellows, *a housekeeper, forty*
Gilbert Shirley, *an explorer and spy, forty-five*
Queen Victoria, *the well-known Queen of England*
A **Savage**
A **Footman**
Two more **Savages**

In Scene Three, the actor playing Lucius will play explorer Gilbert Shirley. The actor playing Lucille will play Queen Victoria. The actor playing Meriwether will play the Footman.

In Scene Seven, the actor playing Lucius will again play the part of Gilbert Shirley, while the actor playing Maisy will play the Savage. The actors playing Lucille and Meriwether will play the extra Savages.

The production is asked to be ambitious in terms of set.
It should be visually bold; it must provide spectacle.

Visually, Scenes Three, Five and Seven do not necessarily need to tally with the rest of the play; however, they must be visually consistent with each other. I suggest an old-style theatrical scenic background, which drops in front of the main set.

The Victorian costumes are largely black, unless otherwise indicated. Only Scenes Three, Five and Seven should be colourful.

Scene One

A large, lonely Victorian drawing room situated in the living quarters on the ground floor of a taxidermy museum.

The stage is covered in as many stuffed animals as possible. Weird and wonderful wildlife from all corners of the globe stare eerily out at us.

Everything looks dusty. The wallpaper is dark. Heavy drapes cover the windows, and all natural light is obscured. There is unnecessary furniture everywhere. Clutter. Claustrophobia. Everything is so typically Victorian it is almost a cliché.

We can hear rain falling heavily outside. A grandfather clock tick-tocks oppressively.

Meriwether *reads from a piece of paper.* **Lucius** *sits.*

Meriwether   'Room One. Aardvark, Cheetah, Gaboon Viper, Long-nose Echidna, Duck-billed Platypus, Red Kangaroo, Night Monkey, Moon Rat, Giant Pacific Octopus, Snow Leopard, Bee Hummingbird, Red Howler Monkey, Giant Panda, Bottlenose Dolphin, Sulphur-crested Cockatoo, Iberian Lynx, Leatherback Turtle, Lion, Emerald Tree Boa, Nile Crocodile, African Wild Dog, Gila Monster, Cape Porcupine, Toco Toucan, Giant Flying Squirrel, Meerkat, Malayan Tapir, Bushbaby, Chinese Pangolin, South American Sea Lion, Swamp Rabbit, Maned Three-toed Sloth, Atlantic Puffin, Bobcat, Aye Aye, Walrus, Water Dragon, Long-footed Potoroo, Narwhal, Lar Gibbon, Snowy Owl, Hippopotamus.

'Room Two. Coyote, Giant Tortoise, Secretary Bird, Dromedary, Wolverine, Goliath Bullfrog, Reindeer, Rodriguez Flying Fox, West Indian Manatee, Spotted Hyena, Eastern Barred Bandicoot, Paradoxical Frog, Burchell's Zebra, Greater Flamingo, Komodo Dragon, Emu, Gharial, Sun Bear, Brown Lemming, Grey Wolf, Hellbender, Cougar, Albatross, Ostrich, Okapi, Zorilla, Koala Bear, Imperial Scorpion, Golden Lion Tamarind, Vampire Bat, Tasmanian Devil, Giraffe, Mandrill, Hartebeest, Serval, Giant Anteater, Emperor Penguin, Bonobo, Great Frigate Bird, Eland,

Plumed Basilisk, Wildebeest, Olingo, Kinkajou, Coypu, Mexican Red-legged Tarantula, Mountain Gorilla.

'Room Three – '

Lucius   Must we continue?

Meriwether   'Room Three. Orang-utan, Capybara, Warthog, Honey Badger, Fire Salamander, Jaguar, Cassowary, Muskrat, Andean Condor, Egyptian Cobra, American Bison, Bactrian Camel, Golden Jackal, Sloth Bear, American Beaver, Polar Bear, Golden Eagle, Pelican, Russian Desman, Dugong, Chacma Baboon, Arctic Fox, Bird of Paradise, Sumatran Tiger, Black Rhinoceros, Giant Armadillo, Chimpanzee.' Correct?

Lucius   Yes.

Meriwether   Quite extraordinary. You have captured God's whole creation.

Lucius   All creatures represent a divine thought. I hope that my collection conveys a small part of His majesty.

Meriwether   Yes. Of course.

He gets out a new sheet of paper, pen and ink.

Name?

Lucius   You know my name.

Meriwether   Name.

Lucius   I do not understand why –

Meriwether   I must follow the given procedure.

Lucius   My name is Lucius Trickett.

Meriwether   'Lucius Trickett.' Your museum has been closed for how long?

Lucius   I don't know.

Meriwether   You must have an idea.

Lucius   I don't know.

Meriwether   Four years. 'Following the death of his wife, Catherine, Lucius Trickett has closed the museum for four years.' I shall write that, shall I?

Lucius   It is your report, Dr Meriwether. You are the physician.

Meriwether   'Following the death of his wife, Catherine, Lucius Trickett has closed the museum for four years.' Correct?

Lucius   Yes.

Meriwether   Four years is a long time to grieve.

Lucius   Perhaps.

Meriwether   How do you feel?

Lucius   Well. Very well.

Meriwether   Your perception of the outside world?

Lucius   You mean do I feel as if I am mad? No.

Meriwether   Please, try to answer the questions . . .

Lucius   How may I measure my perceptions of the external world against those of others? Do you know how?

Meriwether   Well, let's go back to how you feel.

Lucius   How do you imagine that I feel? Am I enjoying this interview? No! These allegations are preposterous. I stand to lose everything that is most dear to me – the museum, my entire collection . . .

Meriwether   I hope that it will not come to that.

Lucius   We are friends, Meriwether.

Meriwether   We have been.

Lucius   Please. For Catherine's sake. You must help me. You must stand in the way of the creditors. Without your diagnosis –

Meriwether   I cannot allow personal history to affect my professional judgement.

Lucius   I have fond memories of you and Emily. I –

Meriwether   Stop. Please. I would like to help you. You know very well how this matter can be resolved.

Lucius   I will not open the museum.

Meriwether   But why?

Lucius   Because I cannot.

Meriwether   The creditors have paid you – they continue to pay you – thousands upon thousands of pounds. It is hardly surprising that they would like the place open.

Lucius   So they claim that I am mad? That I have gone insane? It is abominable.

Meriwether   Emily and the children – they clucked and peeped like little chicks – 'Please say hello to Uncle Lucius.' They whisper to each other about the museum. They presume it a conspiracy of their imaginations. If they could see it again!

Lucius   The museum is closed.

Meriwether   Emily and I pray for you. To lose your wife so young . . . But surely, sir, there is a time when a man must return to his profession, to his life.

Lucius   Catherine was my life.

Meriwether   You refuse correspondence with your closest friends. For four years, you isolate yourself. You hide away in here, with no indication that you will ever open again –

Lucius   I am grieving still! That is the reason, sir, and you may offer that as the explanation.

Meriwether   You cannot live outside life! You cannot escape from the world! You are part of it! You live within it!

Pause.

The creditors have spoken to a maid previously in your employment.

All the maids convey the same disturbing reports. You walk among the specimens all day. You talk to no one. Your daughter is neglected.

Lucius   So I shall lose my life's work on account of a few rumours from the scullery? What will happen to the collection?

Meriwether   Richard Owen will pay the creditors handsomely. They are building a new museum in Kensington.

Lucius   The Natural History Museum? Surely you would not . . .

Meriwether   Do not presume the creditors' patience infinite.

Lucius   And my daughter?

Pause.

How am I to keep Lucille? They would lock her away, without the care of her own father?

Meriwether   I don't know.

Lucius   But this is absurd! I am not mad.

Meriwether   They don't want to hurt you, Lucius. They simply want the museum open.

Lucius   You do not understand. I cannot open it!

Meriwether   Why?

Lucius   I simply . . . I cannot open it!

Meriwether   Why?! In God's name!

Lucius   Because God does not will it! He does not want me to!

A lengthy pause.

I do not accept the teachings of Mr Darwin. I will never open my collection to a London in thrall to this devil's chaplain.

Meriwether   You imply some manner of divine purpose?

Lucius   Well, yes.

Pause.

The more we know about the world, the closer we come to an understanding of the Father that created it.

Meriwether   Perhaps.

Lucius   Our desire for knowledge – its purest form, science – leads inexorably to heaven. We are led to the Garden of Eden by botanists and naturalists, to the holy spheres by our astronomers, by physicians, by surgeons to the seat of our very soul.

But who is the closest to God? The taxidermist! Beasts and birds. New and terrifying monsters. Hundreds of new forms are sent to London every year from the edges of the oceans.

It is the taxidermist who receives these creatures! Every variance of limbs and wings, of fur and feathers signals another leap of God's thoughts. You must have felt it – standing among the specimens.

Meriwether   Yes. Certainly. It's extraordinary.

Lucius   That has been my life. Can you feel it? God is among us! Can you sense Him?

Meriwether   I . . . perhaps . . .

Lucius   I do not suffer from delusions. I have faith. Surely you would not condemn me for that.

Meriwether   No.

Lucius   You have read *On the Origin of Species*?

Meriwether   The men at the club discuss it constantly.

Lucius   You are a religious man.

Meriwether   I have been very much blessed in my lifetime.

Lucius   You believe in God?

Meriwether   Yes, of course.

Lucius   Then you understand me. I must stand firm against this book of Beelzebub, this insidious volume, which pursues logic without logic's centre – the Almighty Father. Darwin robs us of the link between man and God, between God and His very creation.

Meriwether   *The Origin of Species*. I hardly think . . . It explains some oddities of the animal kingdom. That is all.

Lucius   No! If one follows the logic of Mr Darwin, there is no more truth in heaven than in the fantasies of little children! If God did not make us, if He did not create us, then we are not His creatures. We were not made by Him and we will not return to Him in heaven.

Meriwether   My dear fellow, Darwin is widely accepted. You must accept him also.

Lucius   No! For I have been chosen by God to destroy him!

A lengthy pause.

Meriwether   I understand that your faith has been shaken. You're a clever fellow, Darwin does present some . . . challenges. But these are being addressed every Sunday from pulpits across the country – they are being reasoned out. Of course, you hope to see your wife again in heaven.

Lucius   I will see her again!

He is emotional.

Her final promises! Our reunion in heaven! What was that? A lie? Were her last words lies? Was her final breath false?

Meriwether   I did not say that.

Lucius   Please.

Meriwether   I would like to save you, Lucius. But the creditors need a reasonable explanation. Not a discourse on evolutionary precepts.

Lucius   I am trying to explain to you. I am to save heaven and earth.

Meriwether   Thank you for meeting me today.

He goes to leave.

You have been most helpful. Thank you.

Lucius   Wait.

He goes over to a writing desk in the room, and brings out a bound collection of letters.

Don't breathe a word of this to anyone. You're in danger of losing your life if you do.

Meriwether   You are not in any danger.

Lucius   I have not been able to open the museum. I have been in correspondence with a gentleman named Gilbert Shirley.

Meriwether   Gilbert Shirley – this is someone that you see?

Lucius   No.

Meriwether   A voice that you hear?

Lucius   I am not imagining anything. This is a man of flesh and blood. His letters will explain everything.

Meriwether   I do not wish to read them. Keep them. They are obviously dear to you.

Lucius   Three years ago, Mr Shirley was summoned to see Queen Victoria at Osborne House. The letters will tell you all about it.

Meriwether   I'm sorry. This is –

Lucius   You will not have heard his name. He is a spy! Take them!

Meriwether *reluctantly takes the letters.*

Lucille *enters. She is* **Lucius***'s daughter, a sixteen-year-old girl in a wheelchair. She has been listening at the door.*

Meriwether   Lucille?

Lucius   Were you listening at the door?

Meriwether   Goodness, Lucius. She is the exact image of her mother.

Lucius   Go to your room immediately.

Meriwether   It is uncanny.

Lucius   Go to your room.

Lucille   Perhaps, sir. I might speak to you for a few moments. Alone.

Lucius   What?

Meriwether   Yes, Lucille. I would like that.

He looks at **Lucius** – *he wants him to leave. Reluctantly,* **Lucius** *exits.*

Scene Two

Meriwether *is with* **Lucille**.

Meriwether   Well, look at you. You're a young woman.

Lucille   I'm still a girl. I'm sixteen.

Meriwether   You remember me?

Lucille   Yes, of course.

Meriwether   I thought I would not see you.

I brought you some gifts. I left them with Mrs Fellows.

Lucille   You think that my father is mad.

Meriwether   No! Lucille, you must not listen at doors.

Lucille   He is the most brilliant taxidermist in London, in the world!

Meriwether   I'm not trying to hurt your father.

Lucille   Are you aware what an amazing collection this is, Dr Meriwether?

Meriwether   I have followed its progress these twenty years.

Lucille   The specimens are everything to Father. He would be very unhappy if you took them away.

Meriwether   My dear, sometimes people do things which are not in their own interests – do you understand? If your father would agree to opening the building . . .

Lucille   You must wait until I have spoken to him. Will you promise to wait?

Pause.

Meriwether   You remember the maid – Dora Gibbs.

Lucille   Yes.

Meriwether   She is concerned for you. She claims that your father, in the days after your mother's death . . . Has your father looked after you, Lucille?

Lucille   Dora hates my father because he concluded her employment. She would do anything to damage him.

Meriwether   I do not want to believe it. There are other maids – Lucy Sawyers . . .

Lucille   I trapped her fingers in the door and I slammed them again and again until Father heard the screaming.

Meriwether   All the maids tell the same story. They say that you are left alone all day. You are never taken from the museum. You have no company at all. We are all concerned for you. Would you like to be taken away from here?

Lucille *picks up a specimen of a marabou stork. She sits with it on her lap.*

Lucille   Have you ever travelled across the African savannah?

Meriwether   What? No.

Lucille   The marabou stork, the queen of the storks. The largest of all seventeen species. She eats over twenty-five ounces of rotten meat every day. The spots on her face and forehead become encrusted with dried blood. She squirts excrement over her own legs.

Meriwether   It must be the ugliest creature in all His creation.

Lucille   Vultures and hyenas open the thick outer hides. After that she uses her bill like a meat cleaver to carve out chunks. She swallows great big lumps of dead flesh. Eats baby crocodiles, swallows them whole.

Then you see her standing on termite mounds, ingesting whole colonies of swarming stinging insects. She creeps up behind flamingos at the waterside and stabs them in the back with her bill, like an assassin. Then, when there are grass fires on the savannah, the marabou marches in front of the wall of fire, grabbing the terrified animals that are fleeing. She devours them.

Sometimes the storks can't even take off because they've eaten so much flesh. But in the air – goodness, when they are up there! They soar effortlessly a whole mile above the plains. They pick swallows out of the air. Even from the ground you can hear them singing.

I remember your daughter, Dorothea. We used to play together.

Meriwether   Yes, yes. You did. You were very fond of each other.

Lucille   Is she well?

Meriwether   Yes – oh yes. It's all ball gowns, suitors, this or that dance. Father this, Father that. Spiralling round the drawing room carpet like a lunatic.

Lucille   Stanley?

Meriwether   Great big brute. Six foot and he's still going. Chaps at the club call me Dr Victor Frankenstein!

Lucille   Goodness! Six foot!

Meriwether   Lucille, you can tell me if you like. No one will be angry. Are you properly looked after?

Lucille   Have you read many books, Dr Meriwether?

Meriwether   Well, yes.

Lucille   I have read Father's whole library here.

The seafarers of history. They brought tales back from their travels of what they had seen or how they had been attacked. One vessel had seen the tail of a humpback whale rising from the ocean. Another crew had been torn apart by a tiger shark. Another stung by a stingray or mauled by a sea lion.

The amusing thing, Dr Meriwether, the amusing, amazing thing. These seafarers presumed them the same creature. Every animal they saw, every tale that they told, became attached to the same monster. The pictures they drew, an amalgam of hundreds of different ocean creatures. A monster the length of a whale, spitting poison like a sea snake, the jaw of a shark, its neck covered in fur like a bull seal. They saw one monster where there were many. The shape of that creature was not the shape of a real animal at all – it was the shape of every sailor's fear. The world that we see is not the real world at all, we imagine it, according to our fears and our desires.

It's very important that I am with my father. There must be somebody to look after him.

Meriwether   Mrs Fellows!

Maisy *the housekeeper brings in two packages and gives them to* **Meriwether**.

Meriwether   Something for you.

Thank you, Mrs Fellows.

Lucille   Thank you, Maisy.

Maisy *gives* **Lucille** *a filthy look and exits.*

Meriwether *gives* **Lucille** *one of the packages.* **Lucille** *opens it. It is an embroidered white dress.* **Lucille** *laughs.*

Meriwether   You don't like it.

Lucille   I do like it. But when on earth will I wear it?

Meriwether   There will be occasions when . . . Your mother used to wear something very similar.

Lucille   Thank you. It is very pretty.

Meriwether   And . . .

He passes **Lucille** *the next package. She opens it. It is a beautiful pair of shoes.*

Lucille   Dancing shoes!

Meriwether   Dorothea chose them especially.

Lucille   They are beautiful!

Meriwether   You are beautiful. You have your mother's smile. Wouldn't you like to help your father?

Lucille   Could you pass me that?

Meriwether *passes* **Lucille** *a large jar of black paste.*

Meriwether   You may be able to help him.

Lucille   Arsenic paste. It toughens the skin. Look at my hands. The nails fall away. They grow back and they fall away again.

Meriwether   That is the arsenic?

Lucille   Yes. In my museum, I will have a human specimen. I'll rub great globs of paste all over Maisy when she is sleeping. Ever so slowly, her skin will thicken – her blood will slow – she won't be able to breathe. In an hour, she'll be as stiff as one of the specimens.

Meriwether   Goodness, Lucille.

Lucille   I'll undress her, and she'll sit there in the exhibition all fat and red with her big bottom raised in the air. The gibbon, the orang-utan, the gorilla, the bonobo, the chimpanzee. And the prize of the greater primates – Maisy Fellows! Imagine how the public would gape! What an offensive specimen! You must admit – she does eat a lot.

Meriwether   Lucille!

Lucille   After I've scraped out all the entrails, I have to get the skin as tough as it will go, so it's hard like a board. So it hardly feels like there was anything living in it at all. Just the fur and the feathers and the scales. Then you wrap it round the cast as tightly as you can. Sew it all up. It looks like it's alive again!

We were sent specimens for years after the museum was closed. If you don't stuff them quickly they go rotten. And the smell! All these monsters from the Arctic, from the Congo, from islands in the middle of tropical oceans. Maisy wanted to throw them into the street. A hundred pounds' worth of carcasses! My father ignored them, he had shut himself away.

Meriwether   So you . . . ?

Lucille   It's not as hard as it looks. You just can't be squeamish about the blood and guts.

Sometimes you can make your own creatures. It's like pretending to be God. Last year I put antlers on a polar bear. And when Maisy's cat died, I stuffed it and attached the wings of a golden eagle.

Meriwether   Did she like that?

Lucille   No. I once wrote a letter to the Natural History Museum. Richard Owen never replied. I write to everyone and no one ever writes back.

Meriwether   Well, perhaps . . . your gender. It is quite unusual.

Lucille   When I open my own museum, Mr Owen will be sorry. And the rest of them.

Meriwether   Most girls your age are playing the piano.

Lucille   We haven't got a piano.

Meriwether   Or they sew . . .

Lucille   I am sewing.

Meriwether   Embroider I mean. Dresses and so forth. Not . . . animal corpses.

Lucille   Have you ever been to Australia, Dr Meriwether?

Meriwether   No.

Lucille   It is the biggest island in the world, and it is covered in marsupials. Animals who keep their children in pockets.

Meriwether   Do you ever leave the museum? Do you see anyone else?

Lucille   During the week, there are Maisy's children. And I read.

Meriwether   I mean – girls of your own age?

Lucille   No. Why? Do your children?

Meriwether   Yes! Would you like to meet the Meriwethers again? Perhaps you might come and stay for a weekend soon?

He goes over to embrace her. **Lucille** *removes the letters from his pocket.*

Lucille   What are these?

Meriwether   Letters. Your father wants me to read them.

Lucille *is looking at them curiously.*

Meriwether   Your father is not himself.

Lucille   Can I keep these?

Meriwether   I'm afraid I must.

Lucille   What do they say?

Meriwether *takes them back from* **Lucille**.

Lucille   Will you let me discuss the museum with my father?

Meriwether   The creditors are quite determined.

Lucille   I am his daughter. Perhaps you may hold them off until I have spoken with him. You were a friend to this family once.

Meriwether   Well . . .

Lucille   For my mother's sake. Please. Delay your report.

Meriwether *goes to leave. He turns at the door.*

Meriwether   Things may be changing in your life, Lucille. You must not worry. You will be looked after in any circumstance. If your father does not open the museum – you will be looked after. You will be completely safe.

He smiles. He leaves.

Lucille *looks at the shoes.*

Scene Three

The action in this scene should take place in front of a painted scenic backdrop, which falls in front of the main set.

Summer. Osborne House. Bright lights through the windows. The sound of nightingales.

Gilbert Shirley *waits in the gardens. He is played by the same actor as* **Lucius***, but while* **Lucius** *is weak and wild-eyed* **Gilbert** *is effortlessly charismatic and extravagantly moustachioed.*

A **Footman** (*played by the same actor as* **Meriwether**) *with a trumpet appears in the doorway. He plays a regal entrance on the trumpet.*

Footman   Her Royal Highness, Queen Victoria.

Queen Victoria *enters, dressed in her customary mourning. Her bustle is enormous. She is played by the same actress as* **Lucille***.*

Gilbert   Your Majesty.

Queen Victoria   Mr Gilbert Shirley. At last.

She sits. She opens a Bible. She begins to read out loud. After a while, **Gilbert** *joins in, and they reach a loud, triumphant crescendo.*

Queen Victoria   'And God said, Let the earth bring forth the living creature after his kind, cattle, and creeping thing, and beast of the earth after his kind: and it was so. And God made the beast of the earth after his kind, and cattle after their kind, and every thing that creepeth upon the earth after his kind: and God saw that it was good . . . '

Queen Victoria *and* **Gilbert**   ' . . . And God said, Let us make man in our image, after our likeness: and let them have dominion over the fish of the sea, and over the fowl of the air, and over the cattle, and over all the earth, and over every creeping thing that creepeth upon the earth. So God created man in his own image, in the image of God created he him; male and female he them. And God blessed them, and God said unto them, Be fruitful and multiply and replenish the earth, and subdue it: and have dominion over the fish of the sea, and over the fowl of the air, and over every living thing that moveth upon the earth.'

Gilbert   'And God said to . . . '

Queen Victoria   No, that's enough.

Gilbert   Sorry. Sorry.

Queen Victoria   I do not drink since Albert died. But I have some little cakes.

Gilbert   Oooh, lovely.

Queen Victoria (*at the top of her voice*)   Footman! Bring me some of those little cakes that I like!

Footman   Yes, ma'am.

Exit **Footman**. *He returns with cakes.*

Queen Victoria   You have Genesis by heart, Mr Shirley.

Gilbert   Since I was a little boy.

Queen Victoria   We are impressed.

Gilbert   Thank you, ma'am.

Queen Victoria   You got here with no difficulty.

Gilbert   No. I rowed.

Queen Victoria   You rowed here?

Gilbert   It was always a fancy of mine to cross the Solent by canoe.

Queen Victoria   Smooth crossing?

Gilbert   There was a storm. I conquered it.

Queen Victoria   Impressive. Have a cake.

They start to eat. They are clearly nice cakes.

Gilbert   Mmm. Delicious.

Queen Victoria   Mmm. Did you enjoy India?

Gilbert   Yes, very much.

Queen Victoria   I hear reports of man-eating tigers.

Gilbert   Only saw two. And one of them I didn't kill with my bare hands.

Queen Victoria   Then the Congo. The Balkans.

Gilbert   I have beaten bears with clubs, and punctured gorillas with poisoned arrows.

Queen Victoria   Ha! Splendid! Twenty-five missions for us. You have travelled all over the world. From '53 to '55 you were in the Pacific Ocean.

Gilbert   I have unhappy memories of Oceania. I was approaching Melanesia, the black islands. Eight thousand miles from the London winter, where my darling had been taken ill. Brain fever. Illusions. No doctor could help her. I was not able to say goodbye to my own wife.

Queen Victoria   She is waiting for you in heaven.

Gilbert   I know.

Queen Victoria   Albert and I had nine little ducklings. I would that they could be my world . . . but . . . The politicians talk about me in London.

Gilbert   Nonsense!

Queen Victoria   Mr Shirley, you are very kind. But I know that they talk about me. They say that I have gone insane with grief. It is so quiet here. Albert and I used to listen to the nightingales.

This was to be our little vault of heaven, the house. Are you acquainted with the work of Charles Darwin, Mr Shirley?

Gilbert   London speaks of little else. Hooker and Huxley sing his malignant gospels through the length and breadth of God's land.

Queen Victoria   My darling Albert. Beautiful Princess Charlotte taken, just as they imagined God would bless her with an heir. My progenitors, the great Kings and Queens of England. Are we to believe that they are but animals, that they do not now watch over us from heaven, that they do not look upon God's face, their souls complete in His eternal happiness? No, sir! We are created by God, and we will sit beside Him again in heaven!

Gilbert   Amen!

Queen Victoria   Mr Shirley. Have you heard of the ghost loris?

Gilbert   I have heard of the slow loris and the slender loris. The ghost loris – no.

Queen Victoria (*at the top of her voice*)   Footman! Bring me my monkey picture!

You will voyage to the black islands. You will sail back to the darkest corner of the world to find this creature.

The **Footman** *exits and returns with pictures of the ghost loris and maps of a series of islands.*

Queen Victoria   An island in the sun's track, the beating heart of savage land. A jungle infested with poisonous frogs, boa constrictors and cannibals. You will be the first white man to return from the island alive.

Gilbert   I may not return alive.

Queen Victoria   God will protect you on your journey, Gilbert. He will stay the hand of death. For if you succeed – the ghost loris, one specimen of this unhappy creature, will prove Darwin's Theory of Natural Selection specious and return God to His rightful place in men's hearts.

Gilbert   Your Majesty?

Queen Victoria   Yes! This tiny animal provides the key to unlock Darwin's logic. His theory is built upon the 'struggle for life' in which all creatures are engaged. His assumption is that all animals desire life – to mate, to eat, to move. According to Mr Darwin, all creatures lust after every moment's breath. From the lizard, to the monkey, to the man, the craving for existence powers every supposed transformation. We all desire life, above all things.

But consider this, Mr Shirley – we may not all struggle for life. We may not all be designed for the to and the fro, for the bustle of life's relations, this interminable fight for existence. Some of us may be yet alive, but desire to die. Some of us may wait patiently for death. Some of us may no longer want to fight.

She offers the picture to **Gilbert***, who takes it and studies it.*

Gilbert   This ghost loris . . . ?

Queen Victoria   It is a tiny animal, far smaller than the other lorises. Its fur is not brown, but black. In the darkness of the forest, it is almost invisible. A ghost.

Your funny bone. Running down the inside part of a man's elbow is the ulnar nerve. When the ulnar nerve is bumped against the humerus, you have the sensation of bumping your funny bone.

Vital nerves and bones in contraposition can be found everywhere on the body of the ghost loris. When moving in the treetops, it must experience a continuous sensation of resonant pain.

Consequently it spends as much of its life as possible clinging stationary to a liana at the highest canopy of the forest.

Gilbert   It will not move from one position?

Queen Victoria   No. Its whole body is a funny bone! Every time it reaches out to a new liana, its skeleton rings with agony.

And this, the crucial fact. In the forests, the lorises drop from the trees. They perceive the life ahead of them. In one moment they view their future clearly, and they let go of the branches. They drop towards the earth. The forest floor is covered with their little skeletons. They give up, Mr Shirley, they no longer want to live.

The ghost loris holds the key to unlock Darwin's logic.

Gilbert   My God! If I find this animal . . . if this creature could be shown in London . . .

Queen Victoria   You must, Gilbert. You must find a specimen, and dispatch it to the capital immediately.

Gilbert   Your Majesty, I will obtain the animal, or in God's name, die in the attempt.

Shall I send the creature before me?

Queen Victoria   In Camden lives a taxidermist, Lucius Trickett. He has closed his museum and is almost forgotten by the scientific community.

Gilbert   Mr Trickett. Yes. A brilliant man. He exhibited at the Great Exhibition.

Queen Victoria   He has lost his wife and retreated into his own imagination.

Gilbert   He is trustworthy?

Queen Victoria   Yes. He is a true believer. He will not tell.

Gilbert   I will dispatch an introductory letter to Mr Trickett on the instant. I will relate the story of this interview.

Queen Victoria   Good luck, Mr Shirley.

Gilbert   I will conquer it, ma'am.

Queen Victoria   That will be all, Mr Shirley.

Pause.

(*At the top of her voice.*)   Footman! My trumpet!

The **Footman** *brings* **Queen Victoria** *her trumpet and she begins to play, really quite competently.* **Gilbert**, *unsure of what to do, makes his way out.*

Scene Four

We can hear rain falling heavily outside.

Lucille *is out of her chair.* **Lucius** *is holding her in his arms, just as if she were a small child. He strokes her hair and sings to her.*

Lucius
   All things bright and beautiful,
   All creatures great and small,
   All things wise and wonderful:
   The Lord God made them all.

Lucille   When is Dr Meriwether coming?

Lucius   Not yet. I wanted to show you this.

He sets her back down in her chair and uncovers a great big stuffed turtle.

Lucille   A green turtle. *Chelonia mydas.*

Lucius   Exactly right. From the Americas. Isn't it an excellent specimen?

Lucille   Father, I am anxious.

Lucius   I must confess a fondness for turtles. Within this hard head lurks the keenest conception of permanence, of fidelity, in the animal kingdom.

Lucille   You must do something. You will lose the collection.

Dr Meriwether believes that you have lost your mind. He will give the creditors an unfavourable diagnosis.

Lucius   Perhaps.

Every year, each pair of turtles meets on the same beach to mate. Every year, they separate, swim through the world's oceans. The next year, they meet again on the same beach, on the very same day.

Lucille   You have to open the museum. If you don't, the whole collection may be given away. Please, Father! They will separate us!

Lucius   Darling . . .

Lucille   They say you are mad. I know you are not mad.

Lucius   Please don't concern yourself with the matter. It can only upset you.

Lucille   But why?! Simply open the museum, then –

Lucius   Lucille! Your father loves you very much. You must trust him.

The mating partner of this male was killed over fifty years ago. Now, according to local testimony, every year, this same male turtle came to the same beach looking for his dead mate. For fifty years! Imagine it! Every year, a thousand-mile migration. Every year, he travelled across the oceans hoping to see his beloved again! Every year, he arrived, exhausted. He climbed up the beach and waited for her. Every year, he was disappointed. Poor little creature! He came back! Every year he returned, and always in vain!

Lucille   Father, why have you given Dr Meriwether letters?

Lucius   What? What letters?

Lucille   Letters. You have given them to Meriwether.

Lucius   He showed you letters? When? What did you see?!

The doorbell rings.

Lucille   Are they something to do with the creditors?

The doorbell rings again. **Lucius** *kisses his daughter on the cheek.*

Lucius   Good girl. Fetch the Bible, I will come and read to you after Dr Meriwether's visit.

Exit **Lucille***.* **Meriwether** *enters. He is soaked through from the rain.*

Meriwether *removes the letters from his pocket, and gives them to* **Lucius***.*

Meriwether   I came as soon as I had read them. I walked through Regent's Park. It started raining. All at once, a monsoon. Like something out of Humboldt's narrative. It started raining and I laughed. I laughed!

He begins laughing with joy. **Lucius** *joins in.*

Meriwether   Lucius, we are to save God and heaven!

Lucius   You read them!

Meriwether   Yes! Oh, Lucius! That you might be the humble instrument He has chosen . . . Oh, it is a glorious symphony! This man Gilbert!

Lucius   A proper Englishman. He –

Meriwether   The way he articulates his feelings about Darwin. The shipwreck – batted about by the oceans! The escape from the savages!

Lucius   A singular gentleman!

Meriwether   The interview at Osborne House with Queen Victoria herself! A mission from our own monarch!

Lucius   Yes.

Meriwether   Oh, Lucius, Gilbert scratches his pen upon one's very soul. Beside these letters, Darwin's book breaks upon my ears with woeful discordancy.

Lucius   Ha! Yes.

Lucius *and* **Meriwether** *embrace.*

Lucius   You do not know . . . to share this secret after so long . . . your words make me exceedingly happy.

Meriwether   So we, *we*, are to rescue God in the hearts of men!

Lucius   It is quite incredible!

Meriwether   I must ask you . . . You have the specimen? The ghost loris here?

Lucius   It arrived two years ago.

Lucius *goes over to a low cupboard behind an armchair and brings out a sack. From the sack he pulls a tiny monkey-like creature – the ghost loris.*

He gives it to **Meriwether**. **Meriwether** *holds it up to the audience in wonder.*

Meriwether   Emily and I had a little girl. You will recall little Frances. Naughty little Frances! Not much bigger than this creature. In the next life, I will see my girl again. Yes, there is God in every one of us, Lucius. We are His creatures, we come from Him and we will return to Him in heaven!

Lucius   Gilbert Shirley – his brave adventure has saved my life.

When Catherine died, I could not understand God's intentions. I closed the museum, I wandered the floors of the building, looking at the specimens. The more I reasoned, the more Darwin's account of life's beginnings seemed plausible, the more the Bible seemed the less reasonable hypothesis.

I confess that I faltered. Darwin's theory was simple, beautiful, it was completely convincing. It was not God's hand, but this

Natural Selection that had placed us in the world. Millions of
years of tiny incremental change, bound to nothing, to no
meaning except the environment.

The collection led always to God, but now Darwin used these
very same animals as proof against God's existence. These
specimens, my life's work, taunted me. A thousand glass eyes
watched me, they whispered only death. Heaven was a
desparate figment of our imaginations.

I was lost in a dark wood. I had lost the road to God.
Catherine sent Gilbert to save me. Do you understand?!
I might have ended it all! Gilbert brought me back to life.

Meriwether   God moves through us in every waking
moment. No one is forgotten by Him.

Lucius   I wish that I could have told you before. To keep
this secret for so long – you can imagine.

Meriwether   To be part of the divine scheme!

Lucius   I realise I may have seemed . . . eccentric. Now, you
understand. I cannot open the museum – I would draw the
attention of all London. Her Majesty chose it precisely
because it is forgotten.

Meriwether   To think I would have sent an unfavourable
report to the creditors! Thank heaven that I read the letters.

Lucius   Thank you, my good friend.

He embraces **Meriwether** *warmly.*

Maisy *enters.* **Lucius** *jumps in shock.*

Maisy   Brandy, sir.

Meriwether   Thank you, Mrs Fellows.

Maisy   What is that animal?

Lucius   What animal?

Maisy *sets down two glasses and a bottle. She is visibly affected.*

Maisy   Just the sight of it. It goes right through you. What is it? Little monkey thing.

Lucius *moves to hide the loris from her.*

Lucius   You must not mention this animal to anyone. Do you understand?

Maisy   Sir . . .

Lucius   Not even to your husband. Do you understand?

Maisy   Yes, of course, sir.

Lucius   Leave us.

Maisy *leaves.* **Lucius** *pours two brandies.*

Meriwether   Lucius, I must ask you . . . You say the loris arrived two years ago?

Lucius   Correct.

Meriwether   And the last letter came?

Lucius   With the specimen.

Meriwether   Have you heard from Gilbert Shirley since then?

Lucius   No.

Meriwether   You cannot contact him?

Lucius   No. How?

Meriwether   Two years is a long time.

Lucius   He waits for his return on a boat somewhere between Deptford and the black islands.

Meriwether   Consider this, Lucius. The loris reached you two years ago. Gilbert's voyage is long completed. In that time, he may have been shipwrecked, eaten by savages –

Lucius   He may be in the English Channel, waiting to sail up the Thames.

Meriwether   Any number of unfortunate adventures may have come to pass.

Lucius   I have a strong conviction that the man is alive.
I must be patient.

Meriwether   Heavens! It is two years since you received the
loris.

Lucius   God will have protected him.

Meriwether   But what if he is no longer alive?

Lucius   You must have faith.

Meriwether   You cannot simply wait here.

If you were to obtain an audience with Queen Victoria . . .

Lucius   What am I supposed to do? Throw pebbles at the
window of Buckingham Palace?

Meriwether   Scotland Yard?

Lucius   The police? No.

Meriwether   Then there is no choice. Lucius, you must
open the museum yourself.

Lucius   What? I cannot do that.

Meriwether   My dear fellow, it is your duty. You must
present the ghost loris, the theory to London and defeat
Darwin. The response will be most favourable, I am sure.

Lucius   Gilbert asks me to store the creature. That is all.

Meriwether   But it is highly likely that Gilbert is dead.

Lucius   Gilbert is not dead.

Meriwether   But . . .

Lucius   I would not betray my friend. Never! Gilbert saved
my life, don't you understand? He saved my life.

Meriwether   You cannot simply wait . . . I realise you feel
close to him but . . .

Pause.

I have a friend. He has for a number of years been employed by the government in a private capacity. I feel sure he would be able to help us.

Lucius   No one else must know of the letters.

Meriwether   Come, Lucius, you have puzzled over this adventure for too long on your own. My friend is aware of the activities of state. He may be able to find news of Gilbert. He will at least –

Lucius   No.

Meriwether   He will know Gilbert. He may be able to offer advice on his return.

Lucius   An agent of the government? He may be an enemy of the whole project. Our friend was sent directly from the Queen.

Meriwether   Look, we must act. My friend will not tell.

Lucius   I cannot allow it.

Meriwether   But Lucius –

Lucius   You must not tell anyone else about this.

Meriwether *has poured himself another brandy.*

Meriwether   I realise this may not be an ideal time, but I feel I must raise it.

Lucius   What?

Meriwether   I enjoyed my interview with Lucille. She is a sweet, intelligent little girl.

Lucius   Thank you.

Meriwether   Is it natural for a sixteen-year-old girl to be stuffing animals?

Lucius   I'm sorry?

Meriwether   Your daughter's conversation is wild and unruly. On top of it, Lucius, she seems lonely.

Lucius   Mrs Fellows brings her children here during the week. Lucille looks after them.

Meriwether   She has no company of her own age . . .

Lucius   This matter does not concern you.

Meriwether   Nevertheless, I am concerned. I would like her to meet with Dorothea again. It may inspire her to −

Lucius   Your concern does you credit. Nevertheless, I am her father.

Meriwether   The poor little creature. Her little hands are torn to pieces by arsenic.

Lucius   Meriwether, I don't expect you to understand. Girls like Dorothea −

Meriwether   Lucille has many natural qualities.

Lucius   Your daughter is healthy. She hopes for marriage, she will be blessed with children . . . Lucille −

Meriwether   All young women dream of husbands.

Lucius   Dreams that can never be realised! They will become nightmares.

Meriwether   Dorothea is a very caring, God-fearing young girl. She knows about Lucille's difficulties. Next month, at Hanover Square −

Lucius   Completely impossible.

Meriwether   Let me finish!

Lucius   Lucille cannot live in your world. She cannot exist in the society that your children take for granted. They may be amused by her for a while, yes. But my daughter is not a toy that can be cast away when she has ceased to be amusing. You recall your own boy used to laugh at her.

Meriwether   He was a child then.

Lucius   Name-calling. She used to cry all night.

Meriwether   So you will shut her in here for ever.

Lucius   Yes. The museum is completely safe.

Meriwether   It must be a prison for her.

Lucius   And the world a prison outside it. I know my own daughter.

Meriwether   Perhaps you do not know her as well as you imagine.

Lucius   I understand my daughter. Fundamentally. We are creatures of the museum.

Meriwether   I do not doubt that you love your daughter. The way that your love is manifested . . . You treat her like one of your specimens. You trap her in this temple of death.

Lucius   What? How dare you?

Meriwether   I did not want to do this.

I know that Catherine would be devastated to see her daughter locked away in here.

You should be aware that I have not yet written to the creditors.

Lucius   What?

Are you threatening me?

Meriwether   I would like Lucille to come and stay with the Meriwethers. At least until the museum is opened again. Until this whole affair is resolved.

Lucius   You blackmail me? You . . . ?

Bartholomew, my daughter is all that I have.

Please.

Meriwether   I cannot sit here and in good conscience let your little girl rot away among these corpses. I'm sorry, Lucius. I will ask Emily to prepare her a bedroom.

He leaves.

Scene Five

A backdrop falls down. The sea.

There has been a shipwreck.

Gilbert *is holding a plank of wood onstage. He is in the middle of a storm. He is buffeted about by the waves.*

The storm calms. He is stranded in the middle of the ocean. He thinks that he will die.

An enormous turtle passes him. **Gilbert** *grabs hold of the turtle's tail. He is led by the turtle.*

He sees a stork pass overhead. It is not a seabird. He must be near land. The stork's flight leads him to land. He has arrived – the black islands.

Gilbert   The black islands!

Scene Six

The museum. **Lucius** *is agitated.* **Maisy** *enters.*

Maisy   Mr Trickett. If I might 'ave a word. 'S about your daughter, sir.

Lucius   I think she's in her room.

Maisy   I'm very happy for her to look after my little ones. Very happy. Mr Fellows is building the new museum, you know, sir. He's off in Kensington all hours, and obviously I can't have the little terrors under my feet. Sir! I do very much appreciate it, sir. Last night. Three o'clock in the mornin'. We hear something. Screaming. Think it must be cats, it's so loud. Don't know how they do it, they just get this nasty note. Then Edgar says, he says to me, 'That ain't a cat, Maisy. A cat don't scream like that.' 'I think it is,' I says, on account of the note being that nasty note. 'No,' he says, 'listen more carefully, Maisy. Don't rush to conclusions. That ain't the scream of a cat.' You know what? It wasn't. It wasn't even near the noise that a cat would make. Don't know how I got the idea in my head in the first place. That is typical of me, that is. It's our little monsters, isn't it? We rushes in there. Little loves. They're sitting up in bed. Crying and screaming. And I start screaming because they're screaming. Hell of a racket we're making. And Edgar is shouting above it all – 'What's wrong?' 'What's wrong?' 'What's wrong?' Again and again. 'What's wrong?' 'What's wrong?' 'What's wrong?' Aaaargh! 'What's wrong?' 'What's wrong?' 'What's wrong?' 'What's wrong?' I can't hardly hear myself think. Twenty minutes we're at it.

Lucius   If you could come to the crucial point, Mrs Fellows.

Maisy   Some story your daughter told them yesterday were so frightening, they both had nightmares. Woke up in the night hollering. They were terrified. I'm indebted to you that she looks after them. I've said it before, I'll say it again. Only they're at that impressionable age and –

Lucius   What was this story exactly?

Maisy   No use trying to get it out of them. Half-scared half to death they were.

Lucius   Look, Maisy –

Maisy   Only, I thought you'd already told her to stick to spelling and 'rithmetic. We 'ad all that trouble before – remember? Giving the kids these imaginary friends, pretending all sorts of invisible fellows were sneaking up on them at all hours . . .

Lucius   Maisy, Lucille will be staying with Bartholomew and Emily Meriwether. You will have time yet to recover your wits. Your children will forget the story, I'm sure.

Lucille *has entered.*

Lucille   What are you saying, you witch?

Maisy   Do not speak to me! Don't even try and speak to me! Calls me a witch, she does.

Lucille   Go on, get your broom.

Maisy   What?!

Lucille   Fetch it. I'll open a window, let you out.

Lucius   Lucille!

Maisy   I wipe your bloody arse for you, girl! Scaring me kids!

Lucille   Father, this is intolerable.

Maisy   I want to put you on the top of Primrose Hill and let you go. Smash your stupid face in the road. That'd make me laugh.

Lucille   You poisonous old cadaver. You don't know anything!

She suddenly hurls the jar of arsenic at **Maisy**. *It narrowly misses her and smashes onto the floor, covering it in black paste and shattered glass.*

Lucius   Lucille!

Maisy *exits.*

Lucille   Father, I have something to tell you. There is something that I need to say to you.

The doorbell rings.

Father.

Lucius   Go to your room and prepare your things.

Lucille   I –

Lucius   GO TO YOUR ROOM AND PREPARE YOUR THINGS!

Enter **Meriwether**.

Meriwether   Lucille.

Lucille   Dr Meriwether.

Meriwether   Dorothea and Stanley are so looking forward to meeting you again.

Lucille   I am looking forward to seeing them too.

Meriwether   I know Dorothea wanted to tell you this herself. I cannot keep a secret. Next month, in Hanover Square, there is a ball. Dorothea suggested that you accompany us.

Lucille   A ball?

Meriwether   Yes.

Lucille   I have never been to a ball.

Meriwether   Well, soon you shall.

Lucille   Oh, thank you, Dr Meriwether. Thank you. Thank you.

Meriwether   I must speak to your father.

Lucius   Lucille, go to your room and prepare your things.

She exits.

Lucius   If you hurt her, Meriwether, I will kill you.

Meriwether   I would never hurt her.

Lucius   I would not think twice. I would come at you like a savage. I would rip open your waistcoat and eat out your heart.

Meriwether   Come, come, she will be perfectly safe.

Lucius *sinks into a chair.*

Meriwether   You have my word.

Lucius   Your word!

Meriwether   Yes, my word.

Lucius   And what is that worth?

I know you have mentioned Gilbert's letters.

Meriwether   No.

Lucius   You have not mentioned them to anyone?

Meriwether   No.

Lucius   You have not said anything?

Meriwether   No.

Lucius   You're a liar.

Lucius   The ghost loris is gone.

Meriwether   What?

Lucius *goes over to the cupboard. He opens it. It is completely empty.*

Lucius   Empty. Look. The creature has disappeared.

Meriwether   Gone?

Lucius   Stolen.

Meriwether   Stolen? How?

Lucius   Yesterday it was here. Now it is not here. It has disappeared.

Meriwether   Who on earth . . . ?

Lucius   There was a window broken at the back of the museum. I looked for the footprints but there had been a fresh fall of snow. Look at this.

He passes **Meriwether** *a note.*

Meriwether   'This matter no longer concerns you. Return to your life.'

Lucius   I found it in the back of the cupboard.

Meriwether   Who on earth left this?

Lucius   Well, the person who stole the specimen, of course.

Meriwether   Why would they leave a note?

Lucius   Two years of waiting for nothing. Gilbert's voyage completely without purpose. I'm going to ask you again. Did you tell anyone?

Meriwether   I've told you, haven't I? No.

Lucius   Meriwether, you stand in front of me and lie to me.

It is perfectly simple. Nobody knows about the loris apart from me, and you. Either you told somebody, or you yourself have stolen it.

Meriwether   Me?

Lucius   Tell me the truth!

Meriwether   Look, I . . . I may have mentioned the loris in passing.

Lucius   You utter, utter dunderhead!

Meriwether   I'm sorry, Lucius. You may be content to sit in your museum, rotting away. The creditors will not wait for Gilbert for ever. I simply wanted to help you.

Lucius   So you told your government friend?

Meriwether   No one else, Lucius. I promise.

Lucius   Did you tell him who I am?

Meriwether   Yes.

Lucius   And where I live?

Meriwether   Yes.

Lucius   You are unbelievably stupid!

Meriwether   You are too close to the adventure. I thought if we could have another perspective –

Lucius   You told him everything. Well done. Well, did you find anything out?

Meriwether   I made some enquiries. I was very subtle.

Lucius   Did you learn anything – in exchange for all of this information?

Meriwether   My friend was fascinated to hear of Gilbert's mission.

Lucius   Yes?

Meriwether   But he knows nothing about it.

Lucius   It is a secret mission. A secret mission.

Meriwether   He is not acquainted with Gilbert Shirley. He has not heard of his name.

Lucius   He has not heard of him?

Meriwether   No. He thought perhaps if he met you . . . He was very interested. He hates Darwin's theory as much as you. As we all do! He would love to see it fall. I thought he might come here and discuss the matter with you. I told him he wasn't to say anything.

Lucius   Of course he will say! I have kept Gilbert's secret for three years. In one week, you have spread it through the British secret services. Your friend has played you for a fool. Darwin probably has the loris now – oh God!

Meriwether   He was simply excited – he would like to come and look at the loris, that's all. He was enthralled.

Lucius   It is probably already destroyed. Thank you, Meriwether. Thank you.

Meriwether   I don't think he would have destroyed it. Lucius, calm down.

Lucius *grabs* **Meriwether** *round the neck.*

Meriwether   What in God's name are you doing? Lucius!

Lucius   Tell me, Meriwether. Tell me what you know! He must have said more than that. You are keeping secrets from me.

Meriwether *manages to shrug him off. They fight for a while. Neither man could be described as an impressive fighter.*

Finally, **Meriwether** *knocks* **Lucius** *across the room.*

Meriwether   You *are* mad! Tomorrow, I will write to the creditors and give them my opinion.

Gilbert is dead!

Lucius   No!

Meriwether   Gilbert is dead! You have driven yourself insane with waiting. He will never come. Poor Lucius. I did not want to believe that you had lost your mind.

Lucius   You will write to the creditors.

Meriwether   You leave me no choice.

Lucius   My specimens?

Meriwether   They will be taken directly to the new building in Kensington.

Lucius   What about my museum?

Meriwether   I am sorry it has come to this.

Lucius   Lucille?

Pause.

Lucille?

Meriwether   Perhaps when you are feeling better . . . You are clearly in no state to be a father to her.

Lucius   I am not mad.

Meriwether   Catherine was very dear to Emily, and to me. Lucille is a charming girl. She will be very happy with us, I am sure.

Lucius   She is my own daughter. You cannot –

Meriwether   You may have given up on life, but she is sixteen years old! Her life lies ahead of her! It is not reasonable, it is not moral, to let her stay here.

Emily is organising Lucille a welcome dinner. I should take her now. I promise she will be looked after.

Lucille!

Lucille *enters. She is wearing her white dress. She looks suddenly beautiful.*

Meriwether   Darling Lucille, I will wait for you in the carriage.

He kisses her on the cheek.

Say goodbye to your father.

Exit **Meriwether**.

Lucille   Father?

Lucius   Dr Meriwether is waiting for you.

Lucille   Do I look pretty?

Lucius   You look beautiful.

Lucille   Dr Meriwether gave me the dress. He said I looked just like Mother.

Lucius   It is very pretty.

I shall miss you. Very much.

Lucille   Father, I shall scarcely be gone a week!

Lucius   You may enjoy it there. You may want to stay longer.

Lucille *is confused by this. Pause.*

Lucille   Did she go to dances? Did Mother?

Lucius   I met her at a dance.

Pause.

I hadn't danced often before. Your mother was so beautiful . . . I thought my feet might give way underneath me. Her hair. Her mouth. The curve of her back. She was a question, Lucille. And God was always the answer.

You are excited to leave the museum.

Lucille   No.

Lucius   I can see that you are. You must think I am cruel to have kept you here.

Lucille   No.

Lucius   Remember to be careful.

Your mother is in heaven, and she is watching us always. It is for Mother I prefer you in the museum. Do you remember what she was like? She worried when you were outside, she was terrified that you would be hurt.

Dr Meriwether is waiting for you.

Lucille   Father, there is something I must tell you. It may upset you.

Lucius   I am upset already. Well?

Pause.

Lucille   I hope that you will look after yourself.

Lucius   Is that all?

Pause. **Lucille** *approaches with her new shoes.*

Lucille   I cannot fit the shoes myself.

Lucius   Maisy?

Lucille   I told her that you would do it.

Lucius   Maisy!

Lucille   Father, please. It's quite simple.

Lucius *goes over and awkwardly begins to put her shoes on. A long moment between them. Finally, he has finished it.*

Lucius   My little stork. You are leaving the nest.

He kisses her on the cheek.

Do not forget your father.

Maisy *appears at the door.*

The shoes are on. **Maisy** *takes* **Lucille** *away.*

Scene Seven

Again, a backdrop falls in front of the museum set.

We are in the middle of the jungle on an island in the middle of the Pacific Ocean. Howling monkeys scream incessantly. Many other eerie sounds. The lighting indicates bright sunlight. Exhausting heat.

Gilbert (*played by* **Lucius**) *sits on the floor. A* **Savage** (*played by* **Maisy**) *circles him. He is sick from hunger. The sound of drumming.*

Gilbert   Can you hear drumming?

Savage   I can't hear anything.

Gilbert   There. Hear it?

Savage   No.

Gilbert   It's drumming.

Savage   What?

Gilbert   Drumming.

Savage   I can't hear anything.

Gilbert   I'm exhausted. It's so hot in this infernal place.

Savage   You could take off your top hat.

Gilbert   Never! Is there any water left?

Savage   Yes.

The **Savage** *takes out a gourd of water and drains it.*

Savage   It's gone now.

Gilbert   Listen!

Savage   What?

Gilbert   It is drumming!

Savage   You're imagining things.

Gilbert   Can't you hear it?

Savage   Just monkeys.

Gilbert   What?

Savage   Thousands of them. The trees carry on for miles.

Gilbert   It's monkeys who are drumming?

Savage   Not drumming. Calling to each other.

Gilbert   Perhaps there's a hunting party.

Savage   Your mind is playing tricks.

Gilbert   They'd have water. They would give us water.

Savage   Monkeys will not give you any water. Very selfish creatures.

Gilbert   No. I meant a hunting party.

Savage   What?

Gilbert   A hunting party of people. They would give us water.

Savage   A hunting party?! No. That's monkeys.

They listen to the sounds of drumming and monkeys screaming.

We will die in the middle of the jungle. No one will ever find us. Back in your homeland your loved ones, they will never know you are truly dead. They will never bury your body.

Gilbert   I have lived my life invisibly. No one will mourn me.

The **Savage** *has stopped. He rests on a log. He starts to try and sleep.* **Gilbert** *looks round.*

Gilbert   Don't stop.

Savage   We have to sleep.

Gilbert   We have to carry on.

The **Savage** *puts his head down to sleep.*

Gilbert   If I rest then you'll run away and leave me here.

Savage   We're fifty miles from the village. Where would I go?

Gilbert   I have these ink shapes in front of my eyes.

Savage   Fever! Take off your hat.

Gilbert   Never! Do you think if we went in a straight line we would reach the sea?

Savage   No.

Gilbert   If we ran? If we ran in a straight line? How far does the jungle carry on?

Savage   That way – fifty miles. That way – fifty miles. That way – fifty miles.

Gilbert   That way?

Savage   Fifty miles.

Gilbert   Right.

He sits down.

If I could just think straight.

He collapses, exhausted. The sound of drumming.

Savage   I will look after you.

Gilbert   You'll run, or you'll break a branch over my head.

Savage   You can't stay awake for five days. You're beginning to hallucinate. You're in no state to continue.

Gilbert   My name is Gilbert Shirley. My name is Gilbert Shirley.

Savage   Gilbert Shirley.

Gilbert   I am Gilbert. I am Gilbert. I am Gilbert.

Savage   Gilbert Shirley.

Gilbert   That's right. What is your name?

Savage   Jalluishitakitoshoobamboodeedleplafplaf Dinekkistupoobleebleebleebambooneedleplafplaf.

Pause.

Gilbert   It's a lovely name.

Savage   Yes. Have a centipede.

The **Savage** *passes him a centipede. He guzzles it.*

Gilbert   It's disgusting. Are there any more?

Savage   Just one left.

The **Savage** *reaches behind a rock and pulls out an enormous centipede, about as big as a dog. Once set on the ground, it scuttles off into the wings.*

Gilbert   I think I'm beginning to imagine things.

Savage   Take off your top hat!

Gilbert   NEVER!

Savage   You haven't got long left.

Gilbert   God!

Savage   No one can hear you.

Gilbert   God!

Savage   No one can hear you.

Gilbert   Please!

Savage   We will be dead before sunset.

Gilbert   If we stick together.

Savage   I've led us so far into the jungle. You will never get out alive.

Gilbert   I have the heart of an Englishman.

Savage   The tigers will eat that first. They're already circling.

Suddenly, **Gilbert** *has noticed something.*

Gilbert   Look up!

Savage   Why? There is nothing above us.

Gilbert   Look up!

Savage   There is nothing.

Through this entire section, the drumming gets louder and louder.

Gilbert *moves around the stage, like a cricketer in the outfield. Finally, something falls into his waiting hands. The ghost loris.*

The **Savage** *goes to attack him.* **Gilbert** *hits him in the face with his rifle butt.*

Gilbert *takes out a bag. He puts the loris in the bag.*

The **Savage** *is on the ground, wounded.* **Gilbert** *sees him, he circles him. He knows he is on top now, he is enjoying it. He comes up close to him and shoots him in the head.*

Suddenly, an enormous number of **Savages** *run onstage, holding spears.*

There follows a superbly exciting choreographed fight.

During the fight, the backdrop that divides the jungle setting and the set of the taxidermist's museum is ripped apart.

The fight continues in **Lucius**'s *living room.*

Finally, against all odds, **Gilbert** *conquers the* **Savages**, *and escapes with the loris.*

Scene Eight

Darkness. **Meriwether** *manages to switch on the lighting.*

The room is empty. All the animals are gone.

Lucius *observes* **Meriwether** *coolly. There is a change in him.*

Meriwether   Your daughter is well.

Last night before supper, Stanley picked her up in his arms, and twirled her around the drawing-room carpet. She was laughing like it was the most wonderful thing in the world. Oh, she laughed and laughed.

Lucius   Ha!

Meriwether   I wanted to tell you. The ball is this Saturday evening. Your daughter will be making her debut this weekend! The whole of London will be there. She cannot stop asking questions. Who will be coming? What shall I be wearing? You should see the smile on her face, Lucius. You would cross the world to see a smile like that again.

She asks after you. Would you like to come and visit her?

Lucius   No. I know perfectly well I cannot trust you with the care of my daughter

Meriwether   Of course you can trust me.

Lucius   No! You are working for the government.

Meriwether   What? No!

Lucius   Name your friend.

Meriwether   No!

Lucius   Name your friend.

Meriwether   I cannot!

Lucius   No, of course you can't. You see, the reason you are unable to name him has nothing to do with codes of secrecy. It has nothing to do with honour or loyalty, things that you know little about in any regard. The reason that you are unable to name him is that he is entirely illusory. You have conjured him from your own imagination.

Meriwether   No!

Lucius   Nobody could be as stupid as you have pretended to be. You are the spy, Dr Meriwether, operating on behalf of a Darwinist faction in the British government.

Meriwether   This is absurd.

Lucius   Oh, you are clever. I have been your puppet!

Meriwether   This is nonsense. You cannot believe it, surely?

Lucius   How cleverly you have played the dolt and won my confidence! Even though Gilbert had not returned I was a threat. I had the specimen of the loris – an animal with the power to bring down the entire seditious edifice of Darwinism. Now, I have nothing. Should Gilbert return, he returns to nothing. I have lost the specimen, my entire livelihood. You have my daughter hostage and all London doubts my sanity. Yes, I may know about the loris. I may know everything. I would bring Darwin down – but how will anybody ever believe me? I have no evidence, and now I no longer have my word. It is quite brilliant.

Meriwether   No, this is not true. I am not a spy.

Lucius   I hope to prove myself a worthy adversary. You will bring my daughter back to me this very evening. Lucille and I are going on a journey.

Meriwether   What? Where?

Lucius   To the black islands.

Meriwether   What?

Lucius   Tomorrow, we are to board a ship bound for Australia.

Meriwether   Australia?

Lucius   In six months' time, my daughter and I will be on the other side of the world. We will travel to the black islands, navigate high storms, pierce the very heart of that insensate jungle. We will capture another specimen of the ghost loris and return to London in triumph.

Meriwether   What? Lucius, you cannot . . .

Lucius   Your words have no power over me.

Meriwether   This mission. It is madness.

Lucius   You lie. Everything about you is a lie.

Meriwether   Listen to reason, Lucius. You are over forty years old. You have not even left this building for four years, you are in no condition to make a voyage across the world! Even if it were you alone, as a physician I would advise you strongly against the journey.

But Lucille?! It is madness to take her. You would have a wheelchair on a ship? Men die on these voyages. Young, healthy men who are accustomed to sea journeys. Even if you were to reach Melanesia, which is impossible, even then what? You would wheel her through a jungle? You would help her through a forest full of tigers and snakes and all the horror of savageland? It is madness. It cannot happen.

Lucius It has already been decided. You will bring my daughter back to me and we will fetch the loris together.

Pause.

Meriwether There is something I must tell you. I thought that I might not. I know that you feel close to Gilbert.

I am not a spy. When the loris was taken, well – you can imagine – I felt that I had betrayed you, I had betrayed the Almighty Father Himself.

When you gave me the loris, and I held it in my hands for the first time – I knew that it was true. I knew then that I would meet my little Frances again in heaven. We all want Gilbert's mission to succeed.

I wanted to know who had stolen the creature. Then I remembered the thief's note.

Meriwether *holds up the note.*

Meriwether I wrote to my friend on a pretext. I thought I might compare his handwriting with that of the thief. Observe. His hand is not the same.

Lucius *looks. It is not the same.*

Meriwether I continued. I was determined to discover the truth. I wrote to every eminent follower of Darwin. No handwriting matched. Not one hand was the same.

The last reply came in this morning. Charles Darwin himself.

Meriwether *passes him the letter.*

Lucius Darwin?

Meriwether It is not in the same hand. I would have given up. I was furious. I collected my papers. Then . . . Set Gilbert's letters beside the thief's note. Observe the shape of the ink.

Meriwether *hands* **Lucius** *the letters and the note.*

Lucius What?

Meriwether I'm sorry, Lucius.

Lucius   It is the same ink. It is the same hand.

Meriwether   It is Gilbert who betrays you. It is he who has stolen the ghost loris away from you.

Lucius   'This matter no longer concerns you. Return to your life.'

Meriwether   He does not need you. Gilbert has returned to England already. Now, he has the loris.

Lucius   He has the loris. Gilbert is not dead! The adventure is completed.

My dear fellow, I have succeeded in my mission!

Scene Nine

Maisy *comes in. She is covered in snow. The museum has been packed away.*

Maisy   The whole city's covered. Coming down like bed sheets it is.

Lucius   I didn't expect you, Maisy.

Maisy   I wanted to say goodbye.

They say the river's frozen over. All the ships locked in by the ice. The roads are bad. When are you leaving, sir?

Lucius   Tomorrow. Lucille and I are taking the train from Euston. I have an old friend in the Midlands who will take us in. I shall write down the address.

Maisy   Is the little madam back?

Lucius   Her debut is tonight. The ball in Hanover Square. She will be there now.

Maisy   That's a crying shame. I hoped I'd see her.

Lucius   I'm afraid she will not be back until the morning. She is still with the Meriwethers.

Maisy   I hope that you will be well. You and your daughter.

Hesitant but fond, **Lucius** *shakes her hand warmly.*

Lucius   Thank you, Maisy. You have been very good to us.

Maisy   Sir.

She goes to the door, but hesitates.

There's something else.

I was going to speak to your daughter about this myself. I don't want to get her in trouble.

She did love those creatures, you know she did. Not surprising she kept one back.

Lucius   What is it, Maisy?

Maisy *brings* **Lucius** *a sack.*

Maisy   It was underneath their bed. No wonder the poor loves were so scared. Lucille told them to keep it somewhere safe. Told them not to tell anyone. Every night they're screaming for me, every night they have nightmares. It's that animal, that funny animal you had – she told them to put it there.

Lucius *lifts the ghost loris out of the sack.*

Lucius   From Lucille?

Maisy   Who else?

Lucius   From Lucille?

Maisy   Yes!

Lucius *storms upstairs with the specimen.*

Lucille *appears in the doorway. She is dressed in white. She is shivering.*

Lucille   Don't tell him I'm here, will you, Maisy?

Maisy   You're shivering.

Lucille   Father was right. He was right to keep me here.

Maisy   You're meant to be at the ball . . .

Lucille   Nobody even looked at me. They all looked away. They looked straight through me.

Maisy   You're shivering. I'll get you a blanket.

Lucille   I thought at least Stanley . . . He pushed me out on to the balcony. Looking over London. All the lights, Maisy. They were beautiful. I told him about the museum. I told him everything – about Mother, about . . .

Maisy   Poor love.

Lucille   I could see Stanley's breath in the air.

Maisy, it was like being forgiven. To have someone really listen to you at last. I thought he was going to kiss me. I waited. There was a second. A second that I thought that . . .

Maisy   What did he do? He hurt you?

Lucille   No. He left. He had left me there. I turned round to look at him. He wasn't there. He hadn't been listening to any of it. The snow was falling. I couldn't move my chair back inside. It was quite stuck.

Maisy   The arrogant young devil!

Lucille   I was sat there. I could see them all inside. Dr Meriwether laughing and telling jokes. Eating and dancing. Nobody even thought to look for me.

Maisy   In the snow?

Lucille   I almost froze! Dorothea found me and took me inside. I told them all what I thought of them. Them and their stupid dances and ball gowns, their dinners and their parties. You know what they did?

Maisy   Poor creature.

Lucille   They pretended that they didn't hear me. That there wasn't somebody there talking at all. There was just this great silence. And I started shouting, then my voice felt smaller and smaller until I stopped speaking because I couldn't breathe and then when I had finished they continued their conversations, they started eating and smiling at each other again. Like I didn't exist.

Maisy   Lucille . . .

Lucille   Father was right! He was right! I should be in the museum. That's where I belong.

Maisy   Well, you're leaving London now – it'll just be you and your father . . .

Lucius *comes in. He sees* **Lucille**. *He looks furious.*

Lucius   Maisy.

Maisy *exits.*

Lucille   Father?

Lucius   You may have noticed that I've been unusually agitated these past weeks.

Lucille   What's wrong?

Lucius   Last month, something very precious was stolen from the museum.

The question is – how much do you know?

Lucille   I . . .

Lucius   You see, I'm confused.

I was ready to give all this up. I was ready to wash my hands of it.

Lucille   I don't understand.

Lucius   Neither do I. Perhaps you can help me.

How are you connected?

Well?

Lucille   I don't know what you're talking about.

Lucius   Gilbert contacted you?

Lucille   I'm sorry?

Lucius   He asked you to hide the animal?

Lucille   Who's Gilbert?

Lucius   Did he write to you . . . ? Did he . . . ?

Lucille   What animal?

Lucius   The ghost loris!

You have never heard of the ghost loris?

Lucille   No.

Lucius   Liar!

He throws the bag at **Lucille**.

Lucius   I know you're involved somehow, Lucille Trickett.

Lucille *opens the bag.*

Lucille   I can explain.

Pause.

Lucius   Well?

Lucille   I should have let you kill yourself.

Lucius   What?

Lucille   Mother is not looking over you from heaven, she's just dead.

Lucius   How dare you?

Lucille   After Mother died, you shut yourself away. You wouldn't even talk to me.

Lucius   I don't understand.

Lucille   You left me to rot. Your own daughter.

Lucius   You were clever. You could always find things to occupy you.

Lucille   I was a twelve-year-old girl.

Lucius   There were books.

Lucille   I finished them.

Lucius   You learned to stuff the animals that were sent to the museum.

Lucille   I should have let them rot.

Lucius   This is . . .

How are you connected?

Lucille   I'm trying to explain.

Remember when I was little. I used to cry at night. You came to me – never Mother, always you. You used to pick me up in your arms and tell me the most wonderful things, the most wonderful stories. And suddenly I wasn't frightened any more. Suddenly I wasn't sad.

Lucius   So?

Lucille   So I didn't know how to help you. You wouldn't talk to me. And then I remembered what you did when I was sad. I remembered how it felt when you told me stories. I thought . . . I was younger then, I thought . . .

Lucius   I don't understand. This is . . . irrelevant.

Lucille   I wanted to help you!

Lucius   Was there a middleman? Perhaps there was a middleman. Who were you helping?

Lucille   All the animals were arriving. You were letting them rot. A slender loris from Ceylon. There was a mother, and a baby still clinging to its stomach. It was tiny. I thought . . . if I removed the baby . . . changed the colour of the fur . . . if I turned it black . . .

I wanted to tell you. I tried to tell you.

I wrote you letters. From a spy. Gilbert Shirley.

Lucius   What?

Lucille   I thought if you had something to hope for –

Lucius   I'm not stupid, Lucille. Tell me the truth.

Lucille   Father, I wrote the letters.

Lucius   That's impossible.

Lucille   I am Gilbert Shirley.

Lucius   Don't be absurd.

Lucille   You were trapped up there. You wouldn't speak to anyone.

Lucius   If the phrenologists got the chance to look at you, do you know what they'd find? Rubbish. In all the ordinary parts of the brain – rubbish.

Lucille   I wrapped up the creature. I wrote the letters, I put them in an envelope and slid them under your door.

Lucius   Oh yes, and I suppose it was you who met Queen Victoria?

Lucille   No, nobody met Queen Victoria. I just wrote that.

Lucius   Oh, and in the jungle?

Lucille   There is no jungle.

Lucius   Ha! Rubbish. And the Pacific Ocean doesn't exist either?

Lucille   Of course there's a Pacific Ocean.

Lucius   No island?

Lucille   No. Nothing.

I wrote the letters. I made the ghost loris.

Lucius *takes her out of her chair suddenly. He puts her on the floor. She tries to move. She is unable to. She continues to struggle.*

Lucius   This doesn't make sense. You are lying to me.

Lucille   No.

You had lost your faith.

I wanted to help you. If you believed in something. Even a falsehood.

Lucius You?

Lucille You were so sad, Father!

Lucius It cannot be true!

Lucille It is true!

Lucius No!

Lucille I am Gilbert Shirley! I am Gilbert Shirley! I am Gilbert Shirley!

He starts to attack her.

Hearing the kerfuffle, **Maisy** *rushes in.* **Lucius** *stops. He leaves the room.* **Maisy** *puts* **Lucille** *back in her chair.*

Maisy Lucille!

Lucille Go away!

Maisy Lucille!

Lucille Go away! Leave me alone!

Maisy *leaves.* **Lucille** *reaches out to get the jar of arsenic paste.*

Scene Ten

We can see **Lucille** *at the back of the room. She is slumped in her chair, her hair covering her face.*

Lucius *enters. He brings out the loris. He holds it up, its little arms and legs splayed for the audience. A moment of wonder.*

Lucius *turns. He sees* **Lucille**.

Lucius Lucille?

Lucille *remains inanimate.* **Lucius** *goes right up to her face, with his back to us. He holds it. A cry of pain. He lifts her from her chair and walks towards us, broken. Her hair covers her face throughout.*

Lucius drops **Lucille***'s inert body. She hits the ground with a strange crack. She remains curled into the sitting position.* **Lucius** *attempts to pick her up. She remains in this position. She has covered her own skin with arsenic paste. Her body is preserved rigidly in the same position.*

He goes over to the curtains. He opens the curtains. The room is flooded with light.

He goes back to **Lucille***. He lifts her, as a father would a child. He strokes her hair. He sings to her.*

Lucius
> All things bright and beautiful,
> All creatures great and small,
> All things wise and wonderful:
> The Lord God made them all.
>
> God gave us eyes to see them,
> And lips that we might tell
> How great is God Almighty,
> Who has made all things well.
>
> How great is God Almighty,
> Who has made all things well.

The theatre curtains close.